T0031153

JUST A KID FROM MAINE™

by Matt & Stephanie Mulligan

Illustrated by Rick Parker

McSea Books

2022

HIS GRADUATING CLASS SIZE
WAS ONLY THIRTY-EIGHT.

FOOTBALL WASN'T OFFERED THERE
BUT IT WAS NOT TOO LATE!

HE WORKED HARD AND PRACTICED LOTS...

...LEARNING ALL HE COULD...
...AND AFTER JUST
ONE SINGLE
YEAR...

...MATT WAS GETTING GOOD!

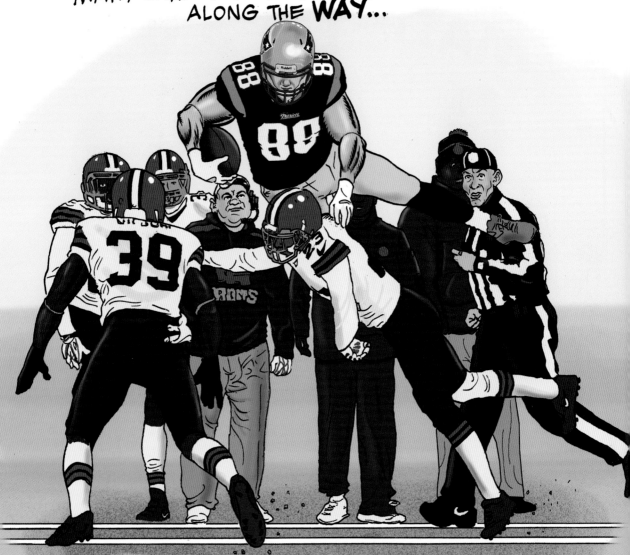

MANY CAREER HIGHLIGHTS MADE MARKS ALONG THE **WAY...**

...BUT ONE VERY SPECIAL MOMENT...

...IS TALKED ABOUT **TODAY!**

...WHEN A KID FROM MAINE --

...WILL CATCH THEIR **DREAMS** ONE DAY!

2021 HALL OF FAME INDUCTEE
MATTHEW BEN MULLIGAN

Born: January 18, 1985, Bangor, Maine
Education: Penobscot Valley High School (2003) | Husson University | University of Maine (2008)

No Mainer who attended a Maine high school has played longer in the NFL than Matt Mulligan. That statement becomes even more impressive when one considers that Matt's high school, Penobscot Valley, did not offer football.

He starred in soccer and basketball and made All-Conference teams.

His football journey began his freshman year at Husson University where he was on the basketball team.

The Eagles were playing Mt. Ida, and the Mt. Ida football team was in the crowd. They looked at Matt's six-four, 260-pound frame and started teasing him. Matt says it wasn't malicious, just fun. "Buddy, you should be playing football!" shouted one of the Mustangs. Matt took the suggestion to heart.

He connected with Husson's football coach, Gabby Price, who put Matt at tight end where he got better every week.

"They let me play, but they didn't ask too much," he told Paul Kenyon of *The Providence Journal*. "They'd say, 'You'll run a corner route' or 'You'll run a seam route.' Then they'd throw me the ball. They didn't even ask me to block."

He would play in seven games and averaged forty yards in receptions per game catching thirteen passes for 282 yards and three touchdowns in the season.

By this time, he loved football.

He was so full of potential. He transferred to the University of Maine where Jack Cosgrove was happy to welcome the strongest tight end in the league. His position coach was former NFL player Phil McGeoghan, who told Matt he had a chance to play in the NFL.

Transfer rules required Matt to sit out a year, which was a blessing. He spent the time learning the game.

"I was so green. I had no idea of any terminology. They'd say things to me, and I'd just look at them with a blank stare. I didn't even really know how to get in a stance."

He would play seventeen games for Maine over two seasons in three years in Orono. He would not be drafted, but many in the NFL were interested in his potential.

He signed as an undrafted free agent with the Miami Dolphins, and the learning process continued. He took the field in 2009 with the New York Jets. He was a third tight end and one of the best blockers in the league.

"Over the near decade Matt played in the NFL, he was by far the best blocking tight end," says his good friend Mike DeVito. The two were teammates with the Jets for three seasons. "Defensive ends and linebackers would purposely line up on the opposite side of the field to avoid Matt. He was one of the strongest, toughest, most vicious tight ends the NFL has ever seen."

Matt is credited with playing nine seasons in the NFL and signing contracts with Miami, Tennessee, New York (Jets), St. Louis, Green Bay, New England, Chicago, Arizona, Buffalo, and Detroit.

He played in eighty-nine games for ten teams, including thirty-one starts. He played in ten playoff games and his teams made it to the AFC Championship Game three times.

Along with being a fierce blocker, he caught eighteen passes for 170 yards and two touchdowns. In 2013, Patriots fans were thrilled when he squeezed a TD pass from Tom Brady, his reaction shown in the picture below.

Now that his playing days have ended, he has most recently taken the position of Strength and Conditioning Coach at UMaine. He also does private consulting on strength, physical conditioning, and wellness through his company, Northern Maine Strength. His clients include individuals, businesses, public agencies such as police and fire departments, and gyms. Matt is an assistant pastor and resides in Northern Maine with his wife, Stephanie, and their three children.

–Bill Green, Executive Director,
Maine Sports Hall of Fame

New England Patriots tight end Matthew Mulligan celebrates his touchdown against the Atlanta Falcons during the first half of an NFL football game, in this, Sept. 29, 2013 file photo taken in Atlanta. (AP Photo/David Goldman)

Stephanie Mulligan grew up in a beautiful village in western Maine and graduated from the University of Maine at Orono with her B.S. in Elementary Education and a concentration in English. She founded the publishing company McSea Books after teaching middle school. She is also the author of *How to Catch a Keeper* and *How to Tap a Maple*. Stephanie lives in Maine with her husband and their darling children. Find out more at stephmulligan.com.

photo credit: Tracie Murchison

Rick Parker was an artist for Marvel Comics from 1978–1996. He is also the artist of MTV's *Beavis and Butt-Head* comic book, the introductory pages of *Tales from the Crypt*, The Pekar Project, and illustrated graphic novel parodies of popular young adult fiction and films, including *Breaking Down*, *The Hunger Pains*, and others for Papercutz Publishing. His artwork has appeared in *The New York Times*, *The Village Voice*, *Time*, *U.S. News & World Report*, *Life*, and countless books by Marvel Comics. His magnum opus, a graphic novel memoir about being drafted into the US Army at the height of the Vietnam War, will be published by Abrams Comicarts in 2022. Rick is married to Maine native Lisa Trusiani, an award-winning children's book author, and they have lived in the Portland area for the last ten years.

photo credit: Jessica Esch

To Dad, Mom and Jared–
I guess all of those whoopie pies paid off!

And to all of my family and friends–
We're stronger than ever before!
– M.M.

To all of my Rhode Island family–
What a great team to be part of.
– S.M.

I respectfully dedicate the drawings in this book to my old childhood
football coach, Luke Sims, who was always fair and kind to me, although
I wasn't a very good player!
– R.P.

Special Thanks to –
Kyle "Just a Kid from Maine" Poissonnier
Owner of Catalyst for Change Wear
www.cfcwear.com

Text © 2022 Matthew Mulligan and Stephanie Mulligan.
Illustrations © 2022 Rick Parker.

This book or any portion thereof may not be reproduced or used in any manner without the express written permission of
the publisher except for the use of brief quotations in a book review.

First Edition

McSea Books, Lincoln, Maine
www.McSeaBooks.com

Printed in China

Publisher's Cataloging-in-Publication Data provided by Five Rainbows Cataloging Services

Names: Mulligan, Stephanie, author. | Parker, Rick, illustrator.
Title: Just a kid from Maine / Stephanie Mulligan ; Rick Parker, illustrator.
Description: Lincoln, ME : McSea Books, 2022. | Summary: NFL veteran Matthew Mulligan of Maine beat the odds with his
outstanding career of nine years as a blocking tight end. | Audience: Grades 1-3.
Identifiers: ISBN 978-1-954277-08-3 (hardcover) | ISBN 978-1-954277-09-0 (paperback)
Subjects: LCSH: Picture books for children. | Football players--United States--Biography--Juvenile literature. | National
Football League--Biography--Juvenile literature. | Maine--Biography--Juvenile literature. | Sports--Juvenile literature.
| Football--United States--History--Juvenile literature. | Success-- Juvenile literature. | BISAC: JUVENILE NONFICTION /
Biography & Autobiography / Sports & Recreation. | JUVENILE NONFICTION / Sports & Recreation / Football. | JUVENILE
NONFICTION / Readers / Beginner.
Classification: LCC GV939.M85 M85 2022 (print) | LCC GV939.M85 (ebook) | DDC 796.332/092--dc23.

Page 16: Cleveland Browns cornerback Joe Haden (23) upends New England Patriots tight end Matthew Mulligan (88)
after a catch in the fourth quarter of an NFL football game Sunday, Dec. 8, 2013, in Foxborough, Mass. (AP Photo/Elise
Amendola)

Page 17: New England Patriots quarterback Tom Brady (12) prepares to throw the ball as Atlanta Falcons defensive tackle
Corey Peters (91) chases and the Patriots offensive lineman Dan Connolly defends during their NFL football game in
Atlanta, Georgia September 29, 2013. REUTERS/Tami Chappell. (Alamy stock image)

Page 18: New England Patriots tight end Matthew Mulligan (88) celebrates with quarterback Tom Brady (12) after scoring
a touchdown in the first half against the Atlanta Falcons during their NFL football game in Atlanta, Georgia September 29,
2013. REUTERS/Tami Chappell. (Alamy stock image)

Page 28 & 30: New England Patriots tight end Matthew Mulligan celebrates his touchdown against the Atlanta Falcons
during the first half of an NFL football game, in this, Sept. 29, 2013 file photo taken in Atlanta. (AP Photo/David Goldman)